11/95

Christmas
in Other Lands

by Janet McDonnell and Jane Buerger
illustrated by Helen Endres

created by Wing Park Publishers

CHILDRENS PRESS®
CHICAGO

Library of Congress Cataloging-in-Publication Data

McDonnell, Janet, 1962-
    Christmas in other lands / by Janet McDonnell and Jane Buerger ;
illustrated by Helen Endres.
      p.   cm.
    Summary: Mrs. Larsen's class learns how Christmas is celebrated in
Mexico, Sweden, Greece, Zimbabwe, and the Philippines.
    ISBN 0-516-00682-7
    1. Christmas—Juvenile literature. [1. Christmas.]   I. Endres,
Helen, ill.   II. Title.
GT4985.5.M33   1993
394.2'6828—dc20   93-7632
                                                      CIP
                                                      AC

It was the last week before Christmas vacation. Mrs. Larsen's class could barely sit still.

"I know you are excited about vacation," began Mrs. Larsen.

"YAAY!" said the class.

"Well, this week we're going to study how people celebrate Christmas in other lands."

"Does everybody celebrate Christmas?" asked Brian.

"No, Christmas is a Christian holiday," said Mrs. Larsen. "It celebrates the birth of Jesus. Not all countries celebrate it.

"But this week, we'll learn about countries that do. We'll go around the globe. And for each place we visit, we'll have a guide to tell us how Christmas is celebrated there. Our first stop is Mexico, and our guide is Carlos."

All of the children were surprised to see their classmate, Carlos, walk into the room wearing a big sombrero. "I'm going to tell you how Mexico celebrates la Navidad. That means Christmas in Spanish," he said.

"In Mexico, they start to celebrate on December 16. That's when the Posada begins. Posada is Spanish for Inn. The Posada acts out the story of Jesus' parents, Joseph and Mary. They searched and searched for a place to stay in Bethlehem. All the inns were full, but they finally found room in a stable with the animals. Baby Jesus was born that night.

"The Posada lasts nine nights. Each night, all of the families in a neighborhood join in a parade. Two children carry statues of Joseph and Mary. Other children carry candles. Everybody sings Christmas carols.

"The parade goes to a different house every night. The people in the house pretend to be innkeepers. When asked if there is room at the inn, the innkeepers say, 'No.' But when they hear that Mary is ready to give birth to Jesus, they let the group in.

"Then there is a party with a piñata. A piñata is a hollow container filled with candy and toys. It can be shaped like an animal, an elf,

or even a star. The children take turns wearing blindfolds and swinging a stick at the piñata. Finally one of them breaks it. Then candy and toys come pouring out."

Carlos showed the class a piñata and pictures from his Christmases in Mexico.

"Thank you, Carlos," said Mrs. Larsen. "Now, tomorrow we'll go across the globe to Sweden, so get ready!"

On Tuesday, Mrs. Larsen's class was even more excited.

"Our guide today is Kiersten," said Mrs. Larsen. "She's visiting us from Mrs. Freeman's fifth-grade class."

"My mother is from Sweden," said Kiersten. "So in our house, we celebrate Christmas the same way they do in Sweden. The fun begins on December 13.

"That's St. Lucia Day. St. Lucia is a favorite saint in Sweden. They say that long ago, she brought food to Christians who were hiding from danger. She wore candles on her head to light the way. On St. Lucia Day, the oldest girl in each family pretends to be St. Lucia. In my family, that's me!

"I wake up very early on December 13 and put on a long, white dress. Then I put a wreath on my head. It's decorated with evergreen and has seven candles on it. When I'm ready, I bring hot coffee and buns to my parents in bed. I have to walk carefully. My little brother and sister follow me. We all sing about St. Lucia.

"Then on Christmas Eve, we have a special dinner, and after dinner we pass out gifts. On Christmas Day, we go to church. When my mother was very little, she used to ride to church in a sleigh!"

Then Kiersten brought out a surprise—St. Lucia buns. They were yellow and delicious. "Yum!" The class gobbled them up right away. Then Mrs. Larsen showed the class the next stop on the globe. "Tomorrow we'll go south, to Greece!" she said.

Merry Christmas

On Wednesday, another classmate, Nicky, was the guide. "Last year at Christmas, my family visited my grandmother in Greece," he said. "Every night, from Christmas Eve to New Year's Day, I went caroling with my cousin and other boys from the neighborhood. People gave us candy, but there were no presents on Christmas. Instead, we had presents and a party on New Year's Day. In Greece, they call it St.

Basil's Day. St. Basil is a favorite Saint in Greece.

"My grandmother baked a cake called St. Basil's Cake, and she baked a coin in it on purpose! She said it was to remind people how generous St. Basil was to poor people. My dad got the piece of cake with the coin in it. Grandma said that meant he'd have good luck for a year.

"Then, five days after St. Basil's Day, we had another celebration. Grandma called it the Blessing of the Waters. The priest led a parade from the church down to the water where there were many fishing boats. He threw a cross into the water. The church bells rang, and the fishermen tooted their boats' horns. Then a

lot of the big boys began diving for the cross. The one who found it carried it through the town, and people gave him gifts. It was fun to watch!"

"Thanks, Nicky," said Mrs. Larsen. "Now, everyone get ready for tomorrow, because that's when we will take a trip to Africa."

The next day was Thursday. Mrs. Larsen introduced the class to a boy named Taj. "Taj is from Zimbabwe. That's a country in Africa," she said. "He's visiting his aunt, Mrs. Freeman."

"In my country, Christmas is a very big holiday," said Taj. "Everyone looks forward to it. The people who live in the bush country get really excited. That's where I live.

"And one day just before Christmas, we go into the town that is nearest to us. We go for a big celebration. People laugh and sing carols, and Christmas lights are everywhere. Best of all, we get to see Father Christmas. He looks a little like Santa Claus, but he is not so fat, and he wears a long red coat. We always stay all night with Grandma. It's fun to stay in the city.

"My father works in town, but on Christmas he comes home for holiday. He always brings bread home at Christmas. Mmmm, I love the long loaves of bread.

"In Zimbabwe, the day after Christmas is also a holiday. It is called Boxing Day. That's because people used to put gifts in boxes and exchange them on that day. But now, gifts are given on or before Christmas.

"Employers always give gifts to those who work for them.

"I think Christmas is fun—both in Africa and here!"

Taj showed the class pictures of his home and family in Zimbabwe. The children had lots of questions for him.

Then Mrs. Larsen said, "Tomorrow is our last stop. We're going all the way over to the Philippines. Then I have a surprise for you!"

On Friday, everyone knew who the guide
would be. Amy had just moved from the
Philippines. She walked to the front of the room
with a red box. She opened it and pulled out
a big, colorful star.

"This is called a parol (pah ROLE)," she said. "It's a star lantern. At Christmas time, you see them everywhere. People put candles or light bulbs inside. All of the kids in school make them before Christmas. I made this one last year.

"In the Philippines, they start to celebrate nine days before Christmas, just as Carlos said they do in Mexico. Each morning people wake up before dawn to go to church. Sometimes fireworks wake them up."

"Fireworks at Christmas?" asked Brian.

"That's right," said Amy. "And on Christmas Eve, they go to church at midnight. Then they

go home and have a big dinner. I always took a nap so I could stay awake late. On Christmas Day, they open gifts. In my family, there was one gift for each person, but it was always a special gift."

Then Amy walked around the room, showing everyone her star lantern.

"Now for the surprise!" said Mrs. Larsen.

She opened the door and in came Carlos with a big piñata! Behind him was Kiersten dressed as St. Lucia. Then Nicky came in with a huge St. Basil's cake. Taj carried a loaf of bread and Amy came in with a star lantern. Last but not least, Father Christmas came through the door!

They had the best Christmas party ever. First they sang carols, then they broke the piñata.

Taj and Nicky passed out bread and butter and cake, and Amy showed everyone how to make a star lantern. Father Christmas even gave the kids little stockings with candy in them.

Mrs. Larsen's class had a lot of fun learning that there are many special ways to celebrate Christmas, all around the world!

ACTIVITIES

An International Christmas Tree

You can decorate a Christmas Tree with flags from around the world. Paint a green Christmas tree on a large piece of poster board, or cut one out of green construction paper. Then color small flags from the countries that Mrs. Larsen's class learned about. Hang them on the tree as ornaments.

Mexico   Zimbabwe
Sweden   The Philippines
Greece

You can add other flags too! They are shown in most encyclopedias.

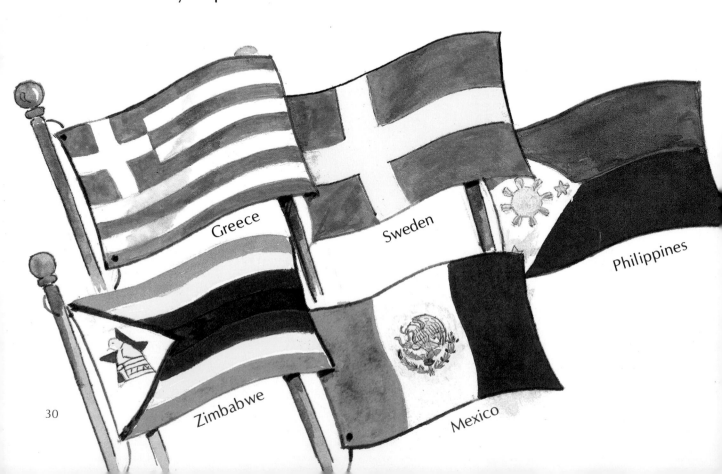

Making Piñatas

To the teacher: 1. Let the children take strong paper bags and 2. decorate them to be piñatas. 3. Then fill the bags with candy and nuts and 4. tie them tightly with heavy twine. Let each child take his piñata home.

If you wish, you can also decorate a much larger paper bag and fill it with candy and nuts. Then you can let the children take turns being blindfolded and swinging at it.

(More elaborate piñatas can be made from papier-mache, and piñatas can, of course, also be purchased.)

It All Means Merry Christmas!

Here is how to say Merry Christmas in the languages of the five countries discussed in the book.

Mexico: Feliz Navidad
Sweden: God Jul
Greece: Kala Christougenna
Zimbabwe: Happy Christmas
Philippines: Merry Christmas

Rice Pudding

This is a special Christmas treat in many countries, including Sweden. Make sure to get help from an adult with this recipe.

Ingredients:

6 ounces rice
1 ounce butter
1 1/2 cups water
3 cups milk
1/2 teaspoon salt
1 1/2 tablespoons sugar
cinnamon
1/2 cups whipped cream
1 almond

1. Rinse the rice in water. Melt half of the butter in an iron pot. Add the water and bring it to a boil. Add the rice, and boil for 10-15 minutes or until the water is boiled away.
2. Add the milk and simmer for 45 minutes, stirring occasionally.
3. Season with salt, cinnamon, and sugar. Add the rest of the butter. Cool. Fold in the whipped cream. Stir in the almond. (You might decorate with red or green coconut or tiny red hearts.)
4. When you serve this, tell everyone that the person who finds the almond in his or her bowl will have good luck for one year!